Exercise!

FLEXIBILITY

Stretch and Move Farther!

Ellen Labrecque

Heinemann
LIBRARY

Chicago, Illinois

www.capstonepub.com
Visit our website to find out more information about Heinemann-Raintree books.

To order:
☎ Phone 800-747-4992
▭ Visit www.capstonepub.com
to browse our catalog and order online.

Edited by Rebecca Rissman, Daniel Nunn, and Sian Smith
Designed by Steve Mead
Picture research by Ruth Blair
Production by Victoria Fitzgerald
Originated by Capstone Global Library Ltd
Printed and bound in China by Leo Paper Products Ltd

16 15 14 13 12
10 9 8 7 6 5 4 3 2 1

Library of Congress Cataloging-in-Publication Data
Labrecque, Ellen.
  Flexibility : stretch and move farther! / Ellen Labrecque. p. cm.—(Exercise!)
  Includes bibliographical references and index.
  ISBN 978-1-4329-6730-7 (hb)—ISBN 978-1-4329-6737-6 (pb) 1. Stretching exercises. I. Title.
  RA781.63.L34 2012
  613.7'182—dc23   2011041323

Acknowledgments
We would like to thank the following for permission to reproduce photographs: Alamy p. 29 (© Eileen Langsley Gymnastics); © Capstone Publishers pp. 15, 17, 19, 21 (Karon Dubke); Corbis p. 12 (© Jose Luis Pelaez, Inc./Blend Images); Shutterstock pp. 5 (© Dmitriy Shironosov), 6 (© tankist276), 7 (© Jules Studio), 9 (© fred goldstein), 9 (© YanLev), 10 (© naluwan), 11 (© Buida Nikita Yourievich), 13 (© T-Design), 22 (© Rob Marmion), 23 (© Orange Line Media), 24 (© iofoto), 25 (© Dan Howell), 26 (© Diego Cervo), 27 (© Fotoline), 27 (© Kai Wong), 27 (© Abel Tumik), 27, 27 (© Elena Schweitzer), 28 (© Alexey Fursov).

Cover photograph of a dancer reproduced with permission of Shutterstock (© AYAKOVLEV.COM).

We would like to thank Victoria Gray for her invaluable help in the preparation of this book.

Every effort has been made to contact copyright holders of material reproduced in this book. Any omissions will be rectified in subsequent printings if notice is given to the publisher.

All the Internet addresses (URLs) given in this book were valid at the time of going to press. However, due to the dynamic nature of the Internet, some addresses may have changed, or sites may have changed or ceased to exist since publication. While the author and publisher regret any inconvenience this may cause readers, no responsibility for any such changes can be accepted by either the author or the publisher.

Contents

The Wonders of Exercise! 4

What Is Flexibility? 6

Stretching Safely 8

Dynamic Stretching 10

Static Stretching... 12

Body Circles 14

Leg Lifts 16

Butterfly 18

Triceps Stretch... 20

Yoga Time 22

Downward Dog... 24

Eating Well.. 26

Big Challenge 28

Glossary 30

Find Out More 31

Index.. 32

Some words are shown in bold, **like this**. You can find out what they mean by looking in the glossary.

The Wonders of Exercise!

Exercise is one of the best things you can do for yourself. It strengthens your whole body. Exercise also makes your **immune system** healthier, so that you can fight off colds and the flu.

Exercise can even help you to **concentrate** better. This means that you can do even better in school by making fitness part of your life.

BY THE NUMBERS

Children should avoid being **inactive** for more than two hours in a row in the daytime.

Cycling is a great way to get exercise.

What Is Flexibility?

Flexibility is how easily your body and muscles can stretch and bend. The stronger and more flexible you are, the better you will be at sports such as gymnastics and soccer.

 You need to be very flexible to do some gymnastics moves.

Being flexible also helps athletes avoid injuries caused by stiff or tight muscles. Let's get more flexible!

Injuries caused by tight muscles can be really painful.

Stretching Safely

Stretching is one of the best ways to become more flexible. Stretching is something you can do anytime and anywhere. But it is important not to over-stretch or to stretch beyond what feels comfortable.

If you feel like yelling "Ouch!" during a stretch, you should stop right away. You should feel **tension** during stretches, but you should never need to shout out in pain.

Stretching should never hurt.

Dynamic Stretching

There are two types of stretching exercises that can help you to become more flexible. The first is when you move your body, or part of your body, while you stretch. This is called dynamic stretching.

 You can move your arms around in circles to stretch your arm and shoulder muscles.

These stretches include sports movements such as a kicking action. This kind of stretch is done before exercise. It helps to reduce the tightness of your muscles.

If you lean on something when you kick, make sure it is strong enough to hold you up.

Static Stretching

The second type of stretching is when your body does not move and you hold the position. This is called static stretching. Static stretching exercises make your muscles longer while your body is at rest. You hold a position (such as bending over and touching your toes) for a count of 15.

Static stretching is usually done after exercise, when your muscles are already warm.

This static stretch helps you to stretch the muscles in your arms.

Body Circles

Body circles help stretch your **core** (stomach), back, and **torso**. Do them as part of your **warm-up**. Spread your feet shoulder-width apart and raise your arms over your head. Lean to one side and bring your arms toward the floor, while bending at your waist.

Continue with your hands moving across the floor to the other side, then upward. Switch directions and do it again.

MINI CHALLENGE BOX

Do this stretch while singing your favorite song. This will keep you moving for longer and also challenge you to keep breathing smoothly.

Type of stretch:
Dynamic stretch

Leg Lifts

Leg lifts help to loosen up your legs. Stand beside a wall and rest your left hand on the wall. Lift up your right leg in front of you, and then move it behind you.

Continue moving your leg forward and backward. Then, turn around and swing the other leg.

MINI CHALLENGE BOX

Do 20 swings back and forth with one leg. Turn around and do 20 swings with your other leg.

1

Keep moving
your leg
forward and
backward.

2

Turn
around and
move your
other leg.

Type of stretch:
Dynamic stretch

17

Butterfly

The butterfly exercise stretches out the inner **thighs** of your legs. Use it as part of your **cool-down**. Sit on the floor with the soles of your feet touching each other and your heels pulled in toward your body. Grab your toes and slowly lower your knees toward the floor. Hold for a count of 15.

MINI CHALLENGE BOX

Try to do the stretch three times, for 20 seconds each time. Take a break in between each stretch.

1

2

Type of stretch:
Static stretch

19

Triceps Stretch

Triceps are large muscles on the back of your arms. They are used in most sports, and it is important to keep them stretched.

Stand with your feet shoulder-width apart. Lift one arm up, bending it at the elbow. Grasp your elbow with your other hand and pull down slightly. Hold for 10 seconds and then switch arms.

MINI CHALLENGE BOX

Try to do the stretch three times for 20 seconds on each arm. Take turns with each arm.

Type of stretch:
Static stretch

21

Yoga Time

Yoga is a type of exercise that helps make your whole body more flexible. People all over the world practice yoga to improve their health and flexibility. It also helps to make people feel happy and peaceful.

People of all ages can learn how to do yoga.

Yoga poses are something you can try, too. You can look online for ideas or go to a yoga class in your area.

Many yoga poses help you to build up your strength as well as your flexibility.

BY THE NUMBERS
About 30 million people practice yoga worldwide.

Downward Dog

The downward dog yoga pose loosens your back and legs. Start on your hands and knees. Make a tall, upside-down V shape by straightening your legs and putting your feet flat on the floor. Relax your upper chest toward the floor until your arms and body are in a straight line.

Take slow, deep breaths when you are in the downward dog position.

Yoga poses can be safer and more comfortable if you use a mat.

BY THE NUMBERS
There are more than 100 different yoga exercises to choose from.

Eating Well

Eating certain foods helps you with flexibility. A diet that includes fruits and vegetables can keep your muscles loose. Eating food that has lots of sugar or salt in it can make your joints stiff.

It is easier to stay flexible when you eat the right foods.

Here is a list of five "super foods" to help you get more flexible:

1. Blueberries

2. Raw almonds

3. Broccoli

4. Green beans

5. Sesame seeds

Big Challenge

The more flexible you are, the better chance you have of becoming a top gymnast. Gymnasts must not only be flexible. They also have to be strong and fast.

To be a good gymnast, you need a combination of strength, balance, and **grace**. If you become flexible enough to bend your body like a rubber band, this will help you with gymnastics, too!

Great gymnasts get to take part in competitions such as the World Gymnastics Championships.

Glossary

concentrate ability to focus on a single task

cool-down last part of a workout when the body is allowed to slow down

core center part of your stomach and back. Your core helps you in almost any movement you make.

grace moving in a beautiful or elegant way

immune system parts of your body that help you fight off illness

inactive not doing anything

tension feeling in the muscles when stretching or straining

thigh part of your leg between your hip and your knee

torso main part of your body. Your head, arms, and legs are joined to your torso.

warm-up gentle exercise at the beginning of a workout

Find Out More

Books
Schaefer, A. R. *Exercise* (Health and Fitness). Chicago: Heinemann Library, 2010.

Senker, Cath. *Healthy Eating* (Healthy Choices). New York: PowerKids, 2008.

Veitch, Catherine. *Gymnastics* (Sports and My Body). Chicago: Heinemann Library, 2010.

Websites
kidshealth.org/kid
This website is devoted to children's health, including exercise, safety, and eating tips.

www.nourishinteractive.com
Nutrition games for kids can be found on this website.

pbskids.org/itsmylife/body/teamsports/article8.html
This website is a great place to learn the basics of gymnastics.

Index

body circles 14–15
butterfly exercise 18–19

cooling down 18
core 14
cycling 5

downward dog pose 24–25
dynamic stretching 10–11, 15, 17

fitness 4
flexibility 6–7, 22, 23, 26
food 26–27

gymnastics 6, 28–29

immune system 4
inactive 4
injuries 7

kicking 11

leg lifts 15–17

muscles 6, 7, 10, 11, 12, 13, 20

safety 8
soccer 6
static stretching 12–13, 19, 21
strength 23, 29
stretching 8–21

tension 8
thighs 18
triceps stretch 20–21

warming up 14

yoga 22–25